MW01094881

How to Get What You Want When You Want It

Overcoming Obstacles to Achieve
Success

Jeff Logue, Ph.D.

ISBN: 1532805578
ISBN-13: 978-1532805578
www.lifenub.com

DEDICATION

To my wife Tammy and my children Ashtyn and Brooklyn.
"Every time I think of you, I give thanks to my God."
Philippians 1:3

How to Get Want You Want When You Want It

CONTENTS

How to Get Want You Want When You Want It

How to Get Want You Want When You Want It

How to Get Want You Want When You Want It

Preface

Amanda jolted awake. Her hand instinctively slapped the snooze button. Through squinted eyes she could see the alarm clock glaring at her. "5:00 AM is too early," she mumbled to herself. She sat on the edge of the bed, preparing herself for the challenging task of standing up. She staggered. Her body ached. Her head was spinning. This was no hangover--just another 20-hour workday amidst a sea of so many others. She stumbled in a sleepy haze toward the shower, then shed her pajamas and stood beneath the tepid water. Her frown indicated a deep resentment at the water for taking so long to get hot. Tears stung her eyes as she began thinking about her life--a single mom, working two jobs, no time for goals or dreams like the girls she worked with. Her bottom lip quivered as she splashed the now hot water in her face, trying desperately to rinse away the luxury of self-pity.

Throwing on her uniform, she dropped two

pop tarts in the toaster, one for her, the other for the sleeping angel in the bedroom down the hall. Coffee in one hand, daughter in the other, Amanda raced out the door headed for the daycare. "Tuition is due today!" she sputtered. As she wrote the check, her chest tightened with anger. Last night's paycheck from *Denny's* didn't even cover daycare fees, much less gas to get to her second job. A Walmart cashier was hardly the career she had hoped for. "I've got dreams and goals too. How am I ever going to get out of this pit?" she lamented.

Amanda's situation is not unique. Most of us have experienced feeling lost in this world at one point or another. We wake up one morning to discover that we no longer enjoy our career. It's lost the excitement that once pulled us from our bed each morning. We look across the dinner table at a spouse we don't like or children that make us weary. When we arrive at work we get a paycheck that fails to motivate us for another two weeks. We feel adrift like a ship at sea. The compass that once drew us toward hope and purpose has long lost its magnetism.

As a mental health professional, I hear so many stories of people who have lost their bearings in their marriage, their careers, and their lives in general. They call and give me a summary of the problem, and we agree on a meeting time to discuss the details. When they arrive in my office, I listen carefully and attentively as they blame everyone for everything wrong in their life. The wife is cold and frigid, the husband is absent and inattentive, the children are disobedient, and the boss is a jerk. If they could just get everyone in their life to change, everything would get better. It's never their fault.

Now, I know that bad things happen to good people all the time. There are usually three sources of pain in this world. First, there is our own self-inflicted pain. Sometimes, we make bad choices and do stupid things that create painful consequences. Take Mitch for example. He was a smart guy in high school, got good grades and was even offered a couple of football scholarships to college. He planned to accept a full ride to college, major in pre-med and become a successful physician someday. That day never came. During his last year in high school he met a college girl who took him on a whirlwind romance. In a few months she was pregnant and his college dreams were gone. They got married, but not because they loved each other. Good people, bad choices. It has not been an easy marriage, but they are still married.

Second, there are "Acts of God." No one can predict an earthquake or where a tornado is going to hit. These are things that just happen because we live on earth. Laura and Jonathan McComb and their two children, Leighton and Andrew, were at a vacation home in Wimberley, Texas, when record-breaking flood waters swept their cabin down the Blanco River. Laura called her sister in the final moment of the

3

tragedy saying, "We are floating in a house that is now floating down the river. Call mom and dad. I love you, and pray." Those were her last words before the house hit a bridge and splintered to pieces. Laura, Leighton, and Andrew perished that terrible day. Jonathan was later found 12 miles away, severely injured with a broken rib, a punctured lung, and a fractured sternum. Some things just don't make sense and beg the question, "Why?"

Third, there are times when we are blind-sided. When I was a child, my family and I were driving down a country road when a drunk driver hit us. Both my parents were killed that day. They had just accepted a ministry position at a church in Killeen, Texas. We were excited about the future; my parents were making plans to minister to military families at Fort Hood. My sister and I were starting to make new friends at school. Suddenly and violently, all that changed. I know bad things happen, and you can be blind-sided by no fault of your own. I lost my parents and my world at the age of six, but I'm still optimistic about the future.

Over the next few pages I want to focus on the first of the three sources of pain. Our choices in life create the majority of our circumstances. In Deuteronomy 30:19 (AMP), God says, "...I have set before you life and death, the blessings and the curses; therefore choose life that you and your descendants may live." Choices create consequences (circumstances) that can lead to prosperity or poverty, life or death, pleasure or pain. If you're feeling lost, it's your fault. You are the navigator. You are holding the compass in your hand. You are the captain of your own ship. It's your hand at the helm. You can blame the wind, the waves, the crew and even the ship itself if you like, but you're still lost. You can blame the system, the "Man," your parents, your boss, even your friends and family. You can blame the economy for a lack of money. You can blame the Democrats, the Republicans, the media or even Bush (everybody else does), but you're still lost. Now, what are you going to do about it? You are the only one who can change your destiny. The fastest way to change your destiny is by the choices you start making right now. Will you choose to keep reading?

1: EXCUSES, EXCUSES, EXCUSES

He that is good for making excuses is seldom good for anything else.

-Benjamin Franklin

When confronted with the previous question, most people start making excuses for why they're not on course. Trust me, I've heard them all. Everybody has excuses. I remember an older gentleman who used to tell me, "Nineteen drops of rain can keep twenty people out of church." Yet those same people will sit frozen, wet and huddled together to watch a Friday night high school football game. Perhaps Benjamin Franklin said it best: "He that is good for making excuses is seldom good for anything else."

What are some common excuses that you like to make?

"I'm waiting for the perfect opportunity." If you're waiting for the perfect opportunity, you might as well quit now. I hate to break it to you, but there are no perfect opportunities. You see, perfection is impossible. It's not in the human condition. We can be great, excellent, outstanding, exceptional, and even

superb; but perfect is not going to happen. As a clinician, I strongly discourage clients from chasing after the perfect anything. It only leads to disappointment. I'm not alone in my opinion. Dr. Paul Hewitt, a psychologist and professor at the University of British Columbia, believes that perfectionism is "a vulnerability factor for ... depression, anorexia and suicide" (Hewitt, 2002, p. 1050).

Another reason to avoid perfection is that it's the lowest possible standard. We know we can't reach it, so we set ourselves up for failure from the very beginning. We get discouraged before we even start. Leo Tolstoy once said, "If you look for perfection, you'll never be content." Don't waste time on things that don't bring contentment.

There is no perfect opportunity. Instead of waiting for the perfect combination of people, timing, and events, take advantage of the everyday events you have the opportunity to use. Remember the story of Blind Bartimaeus? Every day he sat by the road blind and begging for alms from travelers. This day was just like any day, but there was more traffic than usual. He had no idea Jesus would be walking and teaching on his road this day. He had no time to prepare for Jesus' event, but he made the best of the opportunity. All the people hustling and bustling around Jesus didn't stop old Bartimaeus from yelling at the top of his lungs for the teacher's attention.

7

There were even people in the crowd that told him to shut up! He ignored them and yelled all the louder. You know the rest of the story. Jesus heard him over the crowd and healed him. Missed opportunities are not limited to ancient history. The founder of Atari, Nolan Bushness, missed an opportunity to invest $50,000 in Apple. Had he pulled the trigger and taken the risk, he would have owned at least one-third of Apple and be $160 billion richer. Stop waiting for the perfect opportunity and take advantage of the opportunities you have.

"I'm too young" or *"I'm too old."* You're never too young or too old to start doing great things. Don't sell yourself short. Where did you get the idea that you're too young or too old to accomplish great things? Think back to the first time you heard that lie. Where were you? Who said that? What evidence do you have that it's true? History is full of young people who have done great things with their lives.

You need look no further than our own American history to find numerous examples of children and teenagers who left their mark on a nation. Barbara Jones was only 16 when she shut down her high school and created a crisis that ended up in the U.S. Supreme Court as *Brown v. Board of Education,* the case that ended segregation in America. Many remember the actions of Rosa Parks, but few recall that she was inspired by 15-year-old Claudette Colvin, who just a few months earlier refused to sit at

8

the back of the bus. Still not convinced? Let me tell you about 16-year-old Sybil Ludington who helped America break free from Britain's iron fist. You've heard all about Paul Revere and his midnight ride, but Sybil rode that night, too. Charging on horseback through a blinding rain on muddy roads, she let the militias know the Redcoats had breached the Connecticut shoreline. In doing so, the ragtag band of colonists fought back the invasion and drove the Redcoats all the way back to their ships.

History is only one area where we see people too young to make a difference, making a difference. Our world is full of young power players who have made a profound difference in their world. Mary Shelly was only 18 when she penned the classic story *Frankenstein*. Mark Zuckerberg was only 20 when he launched *Facebook*. Andrew Mason was 28 when he founded *Groupon*. Matthew Mullenweg was 19 when he developed *WordPress*. When the Apostle Paul wrote to Timothy, a young 16-year-old minister in Ephesus, he told him, "Don't let anyone look down on you because you are young, but set an example for the believers in speech, in conduct, in love, in faith and in purity" (1 Timothy 4:12). You're never too young to make a difference.

For those of you who think you're too old, you're not. No matter how old you are now, you are never too old for success or going after what you want. Here's a short list of people who accomplished great

9

things after 30:

1. Neil Armstrong was 38 when he became the first man to set foot on the moon.

2. Mark Twain was 40 when he wrote *The Adventures of Tom Sawyer,* and 49 years old when he wrote *The Adventures of Huckleberry Finn.*

3. Christopher Columbus was 41 when he discovered the Americas.

4. John F. Kennedy was 43 years old when he became President of the United States.

5. Henry Ford Was 45 when the Ford Model "T" came out.

6. Suzanne Collins was 46 when she wrote *The Hunger Games.*

7. Leonardo Da Vinci was 51 years old when he painted the Mona Lisa.

8. Abraham Lincoln was 52 when he became president.

9. Ray Kroc was 53 when he bought the McDonald's franchise and took it to unprecedented levels.

10. Dr. Seuss was 54 when he wrote *The Cat in the Hat.*

11. Chesley "Sully" Sullenberger III was 57 years old when he successfully ditched US Airways Flight 1549 in the Hudson River in 2009. All of the 155 passengers aboard the aircraft survived.

12. Colonel Harland Sanders was 61 when he started the KFC franchise.

13. J.R.R Tolkien was 62 when the *Lord of the Rings* books were published.

14. Ronald Reagan was 69 when he became President

of the US.

15. Nelson Mandela was 76 when he became President.

"Aging is not lost youth but a new stage of opportunity and strength." Betty Friedan

"I'm too busy, I don't have enough time." This may be the most realistic of the excuses simply because our lives seem so hectic. Whose fault is that? We all have the same 24 hours. What are you doing with yours? According to Mark Zuckerberg, the average American spends 9 hours a day ingesting digital media. ABCNEWS.com reports that we spend about 40 minutes a day liking each other on Facebook. After that we spend another 5 hours each day watching TV, according to nydailynews.com. Assuming you're getting the recommended 8 hours of sleep each night, you now have only an hour and 20 minutes each day to complete your goals. How's that working for you?

My mother used to tell me, "You always have enough time to do what you want to do." She's right. If you want something bad enough, you'll get it. I started a doctoral program in 2004 determined to get a Ph.D. in counseling. I worked full time, maintained a counseling practice, remained involved in my church, and somehow managed to keep my wife during those five years. You always have time for what you want to do. What do you really want to accomplish in your life?

11

"I'm afraid to fail." Thanks for sharing with the group. It must have taken a great deal of courage to admit that you're just like the rest of us. Fear is proof you're alive. Everyone has fears; most are irrational, but we all have them. John Lennon once said, "There are two basic motivating forces: fear and love. When we are afraid, we pull back from life. When we are in love, we open to all that life has to offer with passion, excitement, and acceptance." The best way to overcome fear is to face it head on. Jack Canfield, author of *Chicken Soup for the Soul*, puts it this way: "Everything you want is on the other side of fear."

What do you want? Is it a six-figure job, your own business, a college degree, or a date with the girl in the next cubical. Climb over that fear and take your dream by the hand and ask her out! When Matt Damon starred in the movie *We Bought a Zoo*, his character Benjamin Mee said, "You know, sometimes all you need is twenty seconds of insane courage. Just literally twenty seconds of just embarrassing bravery. And I promise you, something great will come of it." What great thing are you afraid to fail at? Call it out. I dare you to say it out loud right now.

"I'm too tired." Whose fault is that? What are you doing to contribute to fatigue? What have you done today to prevent fatigue? Put down the candy bar and pick up a peanut butter sandwich on whole wheat bread. For breakfast, introduce foods high in fiber and protein. The fiber will give you energy while the

protein fends off hunger for longer periods. Research published in the *International Journal of Food Sciences and Nutrition* confirms that diets high in fiber contribute to higher energy levels. You mother was right; you should eat your fruits and vegetables. Bananas, citrus, spinach, and sweet potatoes all contribute to higher levels of energy. Couple these with high protein items and you've just increased your energy levels and strengthened your diet.

Take a break from time to time. Sports consultants teach pro athletes to take periodic 5 to 10 minute breaks throughout the day to sustain their energy levels. You may not be a pro athlete, but the principle holds true for desk jockeys like you and me. A human performance study from Louisiana State University, published in *Computers and Industrial Engineering,* found that workers who took four 30-second breaks each hour and a 15-minute break every 2 hours showed higher levels of performance than others.

Oftentimes I hear clients tell me that they are too tired to do anything. I politely disagree and show them the research. For example, a study published in the *British Journal of Sports Medicine* found that mild exercise such as walking, swimming, jogging, and even dancing for as little as 20 minutes at least once a week significantly reduces fatigue. The *American Chiropractic Association* endorses taking mirco-breaks of 5 to 15-second shoulder rolls or getting up and

13

walking a short distance every two hours to alleviate fatigue. A study published in *Psychological Bulletin* found that people with sedentary jobs who engaged in a regular exercise plan reported less fatigue than those who did not exercise.

Maybe you're wondering how you can be tired when all you do is watch TV all weekend. Isn't that resting? Not quite. Watching an entire season of *The Walking Dead* in one weekend will leave you feeling like a zombie, and here's why. Dr. Robert Potter, director of the Institute for Communication Research at Indiana University tells us that sitting around all day slows down our metabolism and circulation. Add to that the emotional and physiological highs and lows that we feel as we watch the zombies chase our favorite characters. This stimulation and arousal can contribute to insomnia and loss of uninterrupted sleep.

"I'll do it later." This is one of the most broken promises in history. We've all said it. We would rather say that than be honest and tell ourselves that we are procrastinating. Most of us laugh it off, knowing we'll get to it eventually. Yet eventually never comes. Tomorrow comes and goes, and the task is still undone. Mark Twain wrote, "Never put off till tomorrow what may be done the day after tomorrow just as well." Twain had a remarkable way of putting a humorous spin on almost anything. Yet for some of you reading this, it's not funny anymore. You're

living on the Procrastination Plantation and have become a slave to fear. I know, the truth hurts, but it also sets you free. Freedom is just a few pages away.

"It's not my fault." This is the excuse that bothers me the most. These four words effectively yield total control of your life to someone else. I hear stories every week from talented and motivated clients who have given control of their lives over to someone else. Millions of people try to live the present from the past. That's like trying to drive your car while staring in the rearview mirror. Millions more allow others to tell them what they are capable of achieving. You can be a victim, or you can be a survivor. You are in control of your present and future. You possess the keys to an engine of achievement that will propel you into greatness. Your success is your fault.

Action Steps

1. What are some common excuses you often use?

2. What are you doing with your 24 hours each day?

3. What do you want out of your life?

2: A POWERFUL WAY OF ACHIEVING GOALS

What you get by achieving your goals is not as important as what you become by achieving your goals.

-Zig Ziglar

When I was a young counselor, I worked in an outpatient community clinic with a number of diverse clients, some of whom faced the challenges of depression, bipolar disorder and even schizophrenia. It was difficult but rewarding work. One of the best lessons my clients taught me was the importance of achieving goals and how empowering it can be. In this chapter you'll learn a powerful way of achieving your goals.

The first step in developing achievable goals is to be SPECIFIC. What exactly do you want to accomplish. It's important to specifically define what your goal is. Stating, "I want to lose weight" is not good enough. In order to be specific you'll need to ask a few pinpointed questions. For example, how much weight do you want to lose? Where exactly do you want to lose the weight? Who else will be involved in helping you lose weight? Why do you want to lose weight? Where will you go to lose this weight?

I teach at a university that has a state-of-the-art exercise facility. It's comparable to any Gold's Gym, and it's only a few hundred yards from my office. To illustrate a specific goal, I might write down the following:

Losing weight is important to me because I want to spend more time playing with my kids and live a healthy lifestyle with my family. Therefore, I am choosing to do 30 minutes of cardio exercise on Monday, Wednesday and Friday from 4:30 PM to 5:00 PM. My goal is to lose ten pounds in the next 30 days.

As you can see, this is a very specific goal. I know why I'm doing it, when I'm doing it, for how long I'm going to do it and where I'm going to do it. This level of specificity takes the guesswork out of getting your goals met.

The second part of setting achievable goals is to

make them *MEASUREABLE*. The first step tells you where you're going, while this step tells you how far you've gone. Think of this step as a map. Before I left home for college, Dad and I sat down at the table and spread out an old paper map of Texas. We didn't have GPS or Google Maps back then. As Dad showed me the route on the map, he took a yellow highlighter and traced the route to college. The next morning when I left the house, I followed the route and knew exactly how far I had traveled and how far it was to my destination.

If you don't know how far you've gone, you'll never know when you get to your destination. Measurable goals help us track our progress. Important questions you'll need to ask along the way are "How will I know when I've succeeded? How much change needs to occur to be satisfied? What do I want my life to look like when I reach my goal? Who else will know or recognize when I've reached my goal? What will I be doing when I reach my goal?" These questions need to be quantifiable. That means there is some way to measure progress beyond your feelings.

When I treat clients with depression, I give them a questionnaire called the Beck Depression Inventory This instrument has several questions on it that are designed to measure symptoms of depression. The BDI has 21 items with a scale that ranges from 0 (*emotion is not at all present*) to 3 (*emotion is very severe*).

19

The BDI includes items such as *Sadness* and *Worthlessness*. There is no universal threshold score to diagnose depression. Higher scores on the BDI indicated more severe levels of this trait.

I then score the BDI to determine the level of depression my client may have. The lower the score, the less risk for depression; the higher the score, the higher risk for depression. I use these scores to measure my client's progress from week to week. By using measurable indicators, I know how they're progressing and, more importantly, they know they're progressing. Sometimes just knowing and seeing progress is enough to break the hold of depression.

Returning to our desire to lose weight, we might use the scales as a way to measure our progress to the target goal. We could also take a closer look at our meal portions or how many smaller meals we eat throughout the day. We could use a stepper and count our steps or the calories we burn. Whatever measure you use, be sure that it's reliable and consistent. If you get discouraged, return to your specific goal and remind yourself of the "why."

The next step to achieving your goals is to pick something *ATTAINABLE.* You may not have been too impressed by my goal in the beginning. Losing 10 pounds in 30 days may not be a big deal for some, according to Fitday.com, but there's a method to my small goal. First, I want to set a goal that is truly attainable. I want you to set a small, doable goal that will give you a sense of accomplishment quickly and with relative ease. I want you to succeed! Second, the thrill of victory will give you the emotional boost you need to set the next goal with confidence.

How do you know the goal is attainable? You'll need to ask yourself a few more questions. Is this goal realistic? Is the time frame reasonable? Do you possess the attitudes, skills, and abilities to reach this goal? I remember working with a client who struggled with schizophrenia. As we sat together, I noticed how well he did while on medication. We talked specifically about some of the goals he wanted to achieve over the next six months. He told me he wanted to graduate from college and become an astronaut for NASA. As we began to look at his goals, we both realized some were not attainable. But I'll never forget the excitement on his face when he enrolled in college as a freshman. Together, we developed a plan to manage his medication, reduce and cope with stress and break down the requirements of his course syllabus.

Now we need to consider if the goal is *RESULTS ORIENTED*. Will the goal, as its written down, produce the results we want to see? Will our weight loss plan get us what we want? Will this goal result in something meaningful to us? Does it help us achieve our life purpose? That may sound like a lofty

21

question, but consider it for a moment. Successful people don't live by accident. Truly successful people plan, strategize, develop purposeful tactics and implement those plans deliberately. They are focused on some meaningful result that will help them achieve their purpose.

Say your goal out loud so you can hear it. "I am losing 10 pounds in 30 days." Let yourself hear it. There are many voices out there talking to you, but the most trustworthy voice is your own. Your voice is the one you hear all day long and everywhere you go. Start stating your goal in the present tense. Blab it and grab it, as the old evangelist used to say. When you say it out loud, it takes on a life of its own. Dr. Ethan Kross, a psychologist at the University of Michigan, discovered that anxious people who encourage themselves using non-first-person pronouns (calling themselves by their first name rather than *I*) tend to perform better in stressful situations. Instead of saying, "I can do this. I can lose 30 pounds" I can say, "Jeff you can do this." Replace *I* with your first name, and your self-talk becomes more believable.

We are creative beings. Create a life for your goal, so it holds you accountable. When I'm really driven to achieve something, I do this and more. I like to tell my friends and family about it, so they can hold me accountable. From time to time my wife and children will ask me about my progress. I've created a group of cheerleaders to encourage me to succeed.

22

They want to see the result as well. My kids will get to spend more time with me as we play in the backyard. My wife will enjoy the benefits of a happy and healthy husband. Results-oriented goals benefit everyone.

The last component of achievable goals is that they are *TIME SENSITIVE*. As a mental health counselor, I've got about three to four sessions to really connect with my client before they choose to continue working with me or terminate our relationship. The first time I meet my client, I want to hear their story and begin to collaborate with them to find a meaningful solution. In this process we're discussing possible goals and action steps to help them reach those goals. Remember I've got about three to four sessions to convince them that our relationship and their investment are worthwhile. Any goals we agree upon must be time sensitive.

Open-ended goals have no urgency. Vague goals cause ambiguity, confusion and a lack of motivation. Set some deadlines that are meaningful and realistic. Tell others about your goal and ask them to hold you to it. If your goal is something like losing weight, invite a workout partner to the gym. The extra company will reduce the boredom of your workout, and the socialization and encouragement will increase your mood. Remember, as iron sharpens iron, so one man sharpens another (Proverbs 27:17). Are there any Iron Men out there?

Let's see what this looks like in the life of John. John has been in the same industry for the last 10 years and feels like he has hit the ceiling financially. For some time now, he has been looking at the skills and experience he has developed and acquired over the years and taking them into a new and exciting career adventure, something different and more challenging but that will allow him to use his strengths and skill base. John is a fairly intelligent guy, so he sits down at the table and begins to develop his SMART goals.

This first thing John does is refine his job search goal by identifying his strongest skills and his deepest values and determining the best culture for him to be successful in by the end of next week. After a few days, he has achieved this first goal by the predetermined date, and now he starts updating his LinkedIn profile to include his skills and improve his professional summary. He completes this is one day. On Sunday afternoon he finds some free time and sends four requests for recommendations on LinkedIn and completes three recommendations from three contacts. In less than a week he has completed three SMART goals. John is feeling really good about himself and his journey toward a new career. Monday morning at work, John discovers that there are several networking events coming up, and he picks one to attend that week. His plan is to get at least five business cards from people he can contact in the new industry where he wants to work. While he waits for the date to arrive for the networking event, he spends his evening completing online applications. His goal is 10 this week. John understands how SMART goals work, and he put them to work for him. Each goal is specific, measurable, attainable, realistic and time sensitive.

Action Steps

1. Pick one goal to achieve this week. You might use the one you stated out load earlier.

2. How will you use the SMART Goals method to achieve this goal?

3: DEVELOPING A MISSION STATEMENT FOR LIFE

Efforts and courage are not enough without purpose and direction.

-John F. Kennedy

Develop a Mission Statement for your life. It sounds daunting, doesn't it? Don't be frightened. Let's take it one step at a time. First, let me explain why a mission statement is important. *Entrepreneur.com* states that "a mission statement defines what an organization is, why it exists, and its reason for being." You have to know what you are, why you exist and your reason for being in order to be successful. Do you know who you are? Who are you really? Stop letting others tell you who or what you are and define it for yourself.

Define Yourself. Stop listening to all the critics, especially the one in your head, and start listening to the still, small voice in your heart. Stop allowing others to build fences around you and box in your creativity. Define your own boundaries and soar over walls that others build around you. Spread the wings of your heart and mind and soar on the winds of possibility.

Decide for Yourself. Why do you exist? This is an exciting part of the process. If you could do anything, what would it be? If you could create your purpose for being in the world, what would it be? In your mind, look over the fence that others have put around you. Turn down the naysayer's voice and listen to the voice in your heart. Why do you want to exist? What is your purpose?

Determine Yourself. What is your reason for being? Why are you here? Determine in your heart why you are here. No one decides that for you. You are in control of this part of your life. Each day you wake up and your feet hit the floor, determine to accomplish your reason for being. You're going to hear many different voices from the crowd below, but determine to listen to the voice that creates your reason for being.

Patrick Hull, of *Forbes.com,* states that "an effective mission statement must be a clear, concise declaration about your business strategy." Let's substitute the word "life" for "business."

An effective mission statement must be a clear, concise declaration about your life strategy."

It sounds powerful, doesn't it? Well, it is powerful. Your mission statement has the power to propel you toward success, and without it you drift aimlessly through life. A purpose statement provides your life with a framework and purpose.

I've seen countless couples in counseling over the years. Without exception, each couple ended up in my office because they either failed to develop a mission statement for their marriage or lost sight of it over the years. A mission statement for your business, marriage or life provides clear, concise, and specific direction during the storms of life. A good mission statement serves as your true North in the blinding storms of life.

Macy's, one of America's oldest retailers, has seen its share of economic storms since it opened in 1858. R. H. Macy failed four times to establish a successful retail store, and later had to file for Chapter 11 bankruptcy protection to survive overexpansion. His mission statement testifies to the retailer's ability to weather economic storms: *"Our goal is to be a retailer with the ability to see opportunity on the horizon and have a clear path for capitalizing on it. To do so, we are moving faster than ever before, employing more technology and concentrating our resources on those elements most important to our core customers."*

In 1886, Richard W. Sears received a box of watches by mistake and began selling them to his friends. The mistake turned into a $5000 profit--a handsome sum for a railway station agent. This son of a bankrupt blacksmith turned a fluke accident into seed money for a $40 million retail giant. The rest is history, but through all that history Sears has held fast to its mission statement: *"We are committed to improving the lives of our customers by providing quality services, products and solutions that earn their trust and build lifetime relationships."*

Henry Ford, arguably the most famous auto manufacturer in the world, began building a motor car for the multitudes in 1907. He was fired from his first job and failed at his first two companies. Yet after two world wars and the death of his own son, Ford Motor Company is still successful today thanks to a strong mission statement: *"We are a global family with a proud heritage passionately committed to providing personal mobility for people around the world."*

You can see from these iconic companies that mission statements provide long-term stability in diverse economic and political climates. I believe the same is true for your marriage, your family and your own life. If you are to achieve great things in life, you'll need a great mission statement for your life. Let's get started on a path toward the future.

Patrick Hull, of *Forbes.com*, suggests starting with four basic questions that I'll modify to help you better develop a personal mission statement.

What do I do? Doing is a big part of success. Action is creative, innovative and imaginative. There is power in action. Active people are powerful agents of change in their family and community. Gandhi said, "Be the change you want to see in the world." Decide what you're doing in your life. Will you be an agent of positive change or negative change?

What do you do? Decide for yourself what this life will accomplish. It's your life and no one can live it for you. No one can tell you what you will do with your life except the person looking back at you in the mirror. My dad told me once, "If you play your cards right, you can be a millionaire someday." Now, I'm not a millionaire yet, but I've made some very wise financial decisions since he told me that. I also need to tell you that Dad never guaranteed I would be a millionaire. He said if I played my cards right something incredible could happen in my life. We are all dealt a hand of cards. Some are dealt a better hand than others. I lost my parents in a car accident at age six. You may still have your parents, but may be overcoming addiction, depression, or bankruptcy. Whatever cards you have in your hand, you hold the cards. Those cards are under your total control. What will you do, hold 'em or fold 'em? What are you going to do with your life?

How do I do it? Once you've decided what to do with your life, you have to figure out how to get it done. Perhaps you've decided to create the best tasting ice cream in America, or design the fastest automobile engine, or just bring about world peace. Whatever it is, you have to decide how to do it. Once

31

you've determined your purpose, now design your process. This is where you define the daily activities that will ensure that you accomplish your purpose each day. What do you need to do to achieve the goal? Keep it simple. It doesn't have to be an elaborate maze of complicated activities. Pick three or four behaviors that you can do each day that will move you closer to achieving your purpose.

Whom do I do it for? Having a purpose and a plan to achieve it each day is a great start, but what will motivate you to dedicate each day of your life to such a mission? What is your why? Who is your why? When I started my quest for the Ph.D., I did it for myself. I wanted to prove to myself that I had what it takes to get the highest degree in my field. To some, this might sound a bit selfish, but I had to decide early on who this degree was for, and my purpose for achieving it. Now I work each and every day for my family. They are the beneficiaries of my hard work. Someday I'm not going to be here anymore, and I want my wife and daughters to be in a very secure place. I want them to be financially taken care of and as secure as possible. To that end, I do what I can to build a financial foundation. As for the present, I'm motivated by a desire to provide emotionally for my family. I want to be healthy and fit so I can model healthy masculinity for my daughters. Eventually, they will marry a man like dear old dad. The interactions a father has with his daughters significantly develop within them a model for the kind of man they will marry. The investments I make into them today will pay dividends 10 and 20 years down the road. Concurrently, the emotional investments I make into my wife pay immediate dividends. What is your why? Who are you living for?

What value am I bringing to others? This is an important question to answer in the process of developing a mission statement for your life. The uniqueness of this question lies in that it is not about you, it's about others. What value do you strive to bring into others' lives? This may sound counterproductive to getting what you want out of life, but I firmly believe that as we give to others, our lives are enriched. To help you complete this step, I encourage you to focus on the following areas.

Focus on the strengths of those around you. It's so easy to complain and criticize those around us, but it's far more productive to draw attention to their strengths. Drawing attention to strengths serves others and offers an alternative to the usual critical climate we inhabit. Most of us are readily aware of our weaknesses and insecurities, but how many people really recognize their strengths? Help your children, spouse, clients, and customers articulate and recognize their strengths. It's so much easier to build upon strengths than to improve our weaknesses. If you're a parent help your children explore where and

33

how they can use their strengths. Children need to feel areas of competence and recognize the benefits of taking the initiative. If you're married join your spouse in exploring new behaviors and skills you can learn together. Perhaps you have a friend who is depressed or grieving a loss; support them in accepting what cannot be changed. I've found in my own life that acceptance can be a powerful form of strength when applied correctly.

Acknowledge and validate others. Many times we walk through life assuming that those around us have it all together and that we're the only ones falling apart. As a clinician, I've learned what to look for in the eyes of the cashier at Walmart or the barista at Starbuck's. The false smile hanging loosely from weary cheeks is a thin mask that does little to veil the lonely sadness. Everyone can benefit from being acknowledged and validated. Successful people are skillful at acknowledging and validating others.

A proper acknowledgement is one that is sincere and specific. Giving voice or recognition to a specific accomplishment your spouse or child achieves is especially powerful. Acknowledging the hard work done by an employee or coworker can make the difference in their life. According to Anita Roddick, founder and CEO of The Body Shop, "The end result of kindness is that it draws people to you." I tend to agree with her, and so does Richard Branson of the Virgin Group when he states, "If people know you care, it brings out the best in them."

What are you doing to communicate that you care about those around you? Any mission worth pursuing must be bigger than your own space. It must include and validate those around you. Oprah once said, "I've talked to nearly 30,000 people on this show, and all 30,000 had one thing in common. They all wanted validation." She powerfully illustrates the need for validation in our society. I wish I could tell you how many clients struggling with problems like anorexia, drug abuse, and depression could have lived different lives if they had had a little more validation in their childhood. Linda Sapadin, Ph.D. describes it this way: "It's getting feedback from others that what I do and what I say matters to you. You hear me. You see me. You think of me. You thank me. You acknowledge my accomplishments. You appreciate my efforts.'" I want to challenge you to validate those around you. Make it your mission in life to validate your children, spouse, friends, family and coworkers.

Stand up for others. We live in a very lonely world. We teach others to take risks, step out on a limb, "climb out of your shell and take a stand," but when they do they are often left standing there alone. I'm reminded of 14-year-old Rebecca Black, who posted a music video of herself singing *"Friday."* The video went viral on YouTube with 160 million views. She was an instant international success because she took a risk. Almost immediately she began receiving hate mail. Here is a little girl who is trying to live her dream, and thousands of people are criticizing her. Rebecca took it as an opportunity to do what she always did, poke fun at herself. She embraced the hate mail and even took a few shots at herself. Never being one to take herself too seriously, she effectively neutralized the haters. It wasn't long until she was sharing the stage with A-List performers like Katy Perry and singing to thousands of screaming fans. Rebecca Black is a success today, enjoying her current YouTube stardom and the adoration of millions of followers. Recalling a conversation with Perry, Rebecca says, "The one thing she told me was never forget where you come from. Everyone knows this industry will rip you and your family apart, just because of how vicious it is. That stuck with me." Rebecca Black was fortunate enough to find a mentor and tap into her own inner strength, but how many people do you know that have been devastated by life because no one chose to stand up for them.

Bullies are everywhere. They're at school, the playground, at work and even online. How many times do we hear on the news about some sweet little girl who is bullied online, her reputation destroyed by the lies of a few classmates, and she decides to kill herself. I recall a scrawny kid with glasses in junior high who was always being picked on and pushed around. He was different, skinny, and clumsy; and to make things worse his voice still cracked. The tough kids at school used to circle around him after lunch like vultures, descending upon him like he was a lamed animal. Girls laughed at him, the teachers overlooked him and he was just a pitiful kid that seemed to attract bullies. One day at one of the bus stops, two upperclassmen got off the bus when he did. While one of them removed a manhole lid, the other stuffed the poor kid down into the sewer hole and ran off, leaving him in there. On a different occasion, he was walking home from the bus stop and two teenagers in a car pulled up beside him and threw red Gatorade on him before peeling off in a cloud of dust and rock that peppered the boy.

I was that boy, and this part of the mission statement is personal to me. No one stood with me when push came to shove. I learned quickly how to defend myself and overcame those challenges by standing up to the bullies. I learned to speak my mind and stand my ground. I learned to use my wits and my fists. I also learned how to stand up for others who were faced with violence. More than once I stood between the bully and the bullied, and the bully backed down.

When we stand up for others, we stand for the possibilities that others want to accomplish. When we advocate for others, we remind them of their goals and the innate power they have to reach them. When we stand up for others, we help to sustain them in

37

their battle for success. When I was in Sunday School, my teacher told a story about Moses climbing a mountain to watch Joshua and the Israelites fight the Amalekites. As long as Moses kept his arms up, Joshua and the army fought successfully against their enemies. But as Moses grew tired, his arms began to drop, and Joshua began to lose the battle. When Aaron and Hur saw this, they rushed to Moses' side and held up his arms until Israel defeated the Amalekites. The story is recorded in Exodus 17, and it's a beautiful illustration of how standing up for others helps the whole nation, community, and family. Standing up for others is a great way to empower others when we remember them, believe in them, hold on to them, and stand with them in the good times and the bad times.

Action Steps

1. What are you doing to communicate that you care about those around you?

2. Review Patrick Hull's, four basic questions and develop a personal mission statement.

4: DESIGN A LIFE OF SUCCESS

…your mission statement becomes your constitution, the solid expression of your vision and values.

-Stephen Covey

As stated earlier, a mission statement defines what an organization is, and why it exists. A mission statement for your life defines what *you* are and *your* reason for being. Once you define *your* life, you must *then* design your life. The word *design* conjures up images of creativity, artistry, and craftsmanship. Drs. Liesch and Finley of Biola University researched the scope, definition, and criteria of the biblical concept of creativity. What they found was fascinating and profoundly important to your ability to design your life. Their research led them to believe that you are endowed with God's creative nature and that creating involves envisioning, fashioning, and linking the product to societal needs. You possess the God-given ability to design the life you've always wanted, and in doing so, provide for the needs of others simultaneously.

Choosing to design your life can be very empowering. Patrick Williams, a successful life coach and author, explains that the purposeful life is not the perfect life. It's a life lived in full awareness of what can be improved, maintained or eliminated. One of the best ways to start the process of designing your life is to use what Williams calls the Life Balance Wheel. Imagine a target consisting of six concentric circles. The hub (innermost circle) of the wheel represents your personal values or mission statement. Now slice the "target" like a pizza into eight pieces. All of these pieces are interrelated and together make up the areas of an ideal life. Williams defines these areas as Career/ Business, Family/ Friends, Finances, Romance/Intimacy, Health, Fun, Spirituality, and Physical Environment.

Give yourself a score of 1 to 10 and shade in the space accordingly. The higher the score in each area, the more ideal your life is. This tool can help you determine what areas of your life need to be improved, maintained, or eliminated. You may also want to record in your personal journal what you want to do to improve your scores in each area.

As you are filling in the scores for each area, list two or three reasons for the rating you've given that area. Next, list at least four actions you can take to improve the rating in that area and how to improve, maintain, or eliminate the reasons for the rating. Let's say that you score a three in the life area of "Family."

Your list of reasons for the rating include the following:

- Wife is angry because I get home late for dinner.
- Children are upset because I'm too tired to play with them.

You might list four or five actions you can take to improve this rating.

- I will call my wife and let her know when I'm going to be home each day.
- I will schedule time each weekend to spend playing with the kids.
- I will use "I" Statements when communicating with my wife to deescalate her anger.
- I will bring flowers home to my wife 1x each week.
- I will seek out my children to validate and affirm them verbally 1x each day.

When filling out the Life Balance Wheel, be specific. Don't analyze your life in a global manner; instead focus on the details of each life area. You may discover that while some areas of your life need improvement, other areas are functioning quite well. Collect all the facts you can from the various life areas so you can compare, contrast and measure your progress. This is not a one-time event. You'll want to revisit this exercise once or twice a month to track the changes and see if you're satisfied and get ongoing feedback about how your life efforts are working. Be careful to listen to others around you. Share your efforts and progress with your spouse and trusted friends. They may be valuable resources for input, feedback and ideas of how to close the gaps. Finally, take the time to evaluate yourself. To design a successful life, you'll need to regularly monitor your habits, beliefs, and behaviors that hinder scores on the wheel.

Action Steps

1. Do a self-assessment using the Life Balance Wheel and take note of what areas in your life need work.

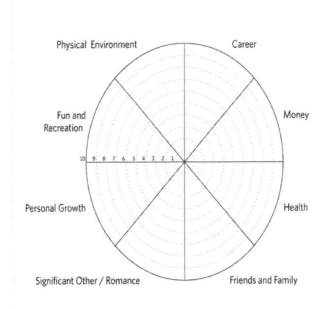

2. Spend some time monitoring your habits, beliefs and behaviors and identify the ones that are hindering your life.

5: SWAT'N SKEETERS ALONG THE WAY

By prevailing over all obstacles and distractions, one may unfailingly arrive at his chosen goal or destination.

-Christopher Columbus

When I was a kid, my brother and I would go fishing out in the bayous just outside of town. We loved to load up the boat and fish until dark in the marsh. We could have fished longer, but the mosquitos (or skeeters as we called them) would move into the shoreline and eat us alive. The fishing was fantastic, but the "skeeters" were such a distraction that we could no longer enjoy the castin' and catchin'.

I've come to realize over the years that life is filled with skeeters that distract us from focusing on our goals. It seems there are a thousand things every day to distract us from what we want to accomplish. You want to be home with your family each night for dinner, but there is a last-minute board meeting, the client that calls just before 5:00 PM, never ending traffic, etc., etc. A few of these skeeters are annoying, but hundreds of them can create a level of suffering that will keep you from enjoying life and reaching your goals.

Buddha said, "Life is suffering." The Apostle Paul told the early Church in Rome, "We rejoice in our sufferings, knowing that suffering produces endurance, and endurance produces character, and character produces hope, and hope does not put us to shame." (Romans 5:3-5, NIV). Sorrow is one of the many common denominators we all share. Regardless of race, ethnicity, or religion, we all suffer from time to time. Suffering is a part of everyone's life. Success is determined by how you respond to your suffering. Its best to embrace it, push through it and recognize the life-changing qualities found in suffering. Paul was right in his understanding of suffering; it produces endurance, character and hope.

Although we cannot eliminate all suffering, nor should we, you can evaluate your life and begin to identify those skeeters that can be eliminated. Take the time to identify the skeeters that waste your time at work. Set your computer tool bar to "busy" so you're not distracted by instant messaging. Email is convenient but not very efficient when you can call the other person and knock out a whole conversation in a few minutes instead of drawing it out over several hours and multiple emails. Meetings are important but can be a serious waste of time if nothing is accomplished. Meetings should be streamlined so that members keep to the agenda and discussion is goal directed. Consider whether you need a meeting or if the topic can be taken care of with a group email.

Tania Khadder of *Insideteck.monster.com* says that the average employee is interrupted every 11 minutes. The emails, the phone calls, and the nosy coworker can all be managed successfully. Decide to answer email twice a day (morning and afternoon), let your phone calls go to voicemail, and let coworkers know that you're busy and you will catch up with them at lunch. Stop multitasking. If you're trying to do everything, you're probably not doing anything very well. Start the day by prioritizing tasks and complete them in order of importance. You'll do a better job, because your full attention is on one project at a time. This will also help you swat the next skeeter--clutter. De-clutter your life at work by cleaning off your desk at the end of each day. De-clutter your closet by going through and cleaning it out so you can make $500 in a garage sale. De-clutter your marriage by setting down with your spouse, apologizing and asking them to forgive you. Declutter your family by sitting down with your kids and planning an activity with them, shooting hoops, or reading them a story. You'll be amazed at how this changes your relationship with your children. You'll spend less time clashing and more time laughing.

It is so easy to stay connected to family, friends and clients now with Twitter, Facebook, Instagram, etc. These are great tools, but they can also be pesky skeeters buzzing around distracting you from your success. Rebecca Hiscott of the *Huffington Post.com*, found that surfing Facebook contributes to lower moods. This same idea is supported by Christina DesMarais of *Inc.com*, who goes further by saying it contributes to depression and depression leads to lower productivity at work. Lower productivity can jeopardize your job. I recently spoke to a woman whose boss fired several employees for surfing Facebook while on the clock. She was terrified of losing her job since she was guilty of doing the same thing. That skeeter almost cost her a career.

Another skeeter is complacency. Webster defines complacency as a feeling of being satisfied with the way things are and not wanting to change them for the better. What a terrible place to be! Satisfaction can be very dangerous to personal development. When the hare became satisfied with his performance, he lost the race to the tortoise.

48

Ronald Reagan once said, "History will record with the greatest astonishment that those who had the most to lose did the least to prevent its happening." Don't be that guy. Complacency comes disguised as self-satisfaction, but later reveals itself as a dangerous unawareness of deficiencies. Looking back at pre-war Germany, history show us how a collective complacency and self-satisfaction paved the road for Hitler's Nazi atrocities. The complacent person never recognizes their own current condition.

A skeeter can come in the form of a negative mindset. This is the belief that you cannot change. How terrifying! Yet, you may be saying that to yourself right now. Whatever you think about the longest becomes the strongest. That may sound simple, but it really is just that simple. Sometimes we need to purge our minds and change the filter. I recently had to repair my garbage disposal. It had become clogged and stopped working. After several minutes of inspection, I finally had to reach inside and dig out the nasty, slimy gunk clogging it. What do you need to dig out of your thoughts to get your mind working in the right direction?

Another skeeter is guilt, usually about something in our past. All of us have made mistakes in the past that we regret. Guilt can catapult you toward making amends for your wrongs, or it can be a yoke around your neck that hinders your potential success in life. What guilt becomes is up to you.

49

Living a life of success and achievement is all about looking ahead rather than behind. You cannot change your past or the guilt you may feel about your mistakes. You can turn that guilt into fuel that propels you beyond regret and shame. The past influences your present, but it does not have to determine your future. You, not your past, determine your present and future success. Get off your guilt and unwrap your present; there is a beautiful future inside. Stop swatin' skeeters and achieve your goals.

Action Steps

1. What are the most common "Skeeters" that distract you from your goals?

2. What areas of your life need to be de-cluttered?

3. How might you have become complacent in life?

6: HOW TO KEEP GETTING WHAT YOU WANT

The starting point of all achievement is desire.
-   Napoleon Hill

Erik Weihenmayer, an athlete, adventurer, author, activist, motivational speaker, and, on May 25, 2001, the only blind person to reach the summit of Mount Everest was not satisfied with those small goals. He understood, as he put it, "the spark of greatness in all people," and he launched himself toward another tremendous achievement, solo kayaking 277 miles through the Grand Canyon. He completed his adventure on September 28, 2014.

There is nothing quite like achieving your goals. Achievement, like any mountain peak experience, requires that we take time to reflect on the events that brought us to the summit. It's important to take a breath and look around once you reach the top. Admire the view, enjoy the thrill of victory, and honor those that helped you reach the top. In doing so, you may discover the key to always getting what you want out of life. I believe the people who keep getting what they want in life have three specific characteristics.

Successful people have consistent focus. Nothing deters them from the goal on which they are focused. Jack Canfield once said, "Successful people maintain a positive focus in life no matter what is going on around them. They stay focused on their past successes rather than their past failures, and on the next action steps they need to take to get them closer to the fulfillment of their goals rather than all the other distractions that life presents to them." Their consistent focus determines their future steps.

Think back to your most recent success. Did anything deter you from achieving your goal? Perhaps while others were drinking at the party, your consistent focus was on sobriety. Maybe while others were getting a second helping of Christmas dinner, you held back and focused on that new bikini you wanted to buy. You may be the one paying cash for purchases while your friends are swiping their credit cards. Whatever your last achievement, you did it with consistent focus on the goal. Alexander Graham Bell said, "Concentrate all your thoughts upon the

53

work at hand. The sun's rays do not burn until brought to a focus." Consistent focus is critical to getting what you want in life.

Part of that success comes from focusing on the future. Oftentimes we spend precious time and effort looking back at our past mistakes and catastrophizing them. When the Apostle Paul was facing persecution in his effort to establish the early Christian church, his energy focused on forgetting the past and pressing on toward the highest prize--God's will for his life. This was no small task. He stood up to the Roman government and suffered severe persecution (2 Corinthians 11:23-28). How were he and others able to continue their race toward the goal? Consistent focus!

We often focus too much on the process and not on the benefit. We get lost in the pain, sacrifice, time and effort it takes to achieve great things in this life. Truly successful people keep consistent focus on the benefits earned as a result of the process. Think about who benefits from your success. When you succeed as a small business owner, each of your employees benefits from your success. When your marriage succeeds, your children benefit from a happy and healthy home. When your ministry succeeds, countless people in your community benefit from your success. Success is a gift you give to yourself and those around you each day you engage in consistent focus.

Another characteristic of people who keep

getting what they want is consistent action. Successful people do something. They are active on purpose. Their days are planned with action steps that lead toward their goals. Their thoughts are action oriented and lead toward greater achievements each day. They are "action-ated" and infused with goal-directed energy that cannot be thwarted by the common distractions of the day.

Successful people learn the power of NOW. Stop waiting for your big chance, and do it now. Don't give opportunity a chance to knock twice; run down the street and find it. Better yet, create the opportunity you're looking for. Stop standing at the punch bowl waiting for the cute girl to talk to you. Pour her a drink, walk across the dance floor and introduce yourself.

Successful people don't wait for tomorrow, they seize the day and achieve great things. When are you going to start? Nothing happens until you start. Saint Francis of Assisi said, "Start by doing what's necessary; then do what's possible; and suddenly you are doing the impossible." What an amazing formula for success. What are the necessary things that must be done in your life, your family, your marriage or your business? They are usually the biggest obstacles to your success. Name them out loud, write them down, and take care of them. Do they seem impossible? Start with what you can do, the possible. Pick up the phone and apologize to your spouse. Take your daughter out for ice cream and tell her you love her. Bring your wife some flowers. Before you know it, the impossible will be your reality.

It really *is* that simple. The hardest part is deciding to do it. You must do it. Whatever you make a MUST will happen. You must breathe, and you will. You must drink water, and you will. You must eat, and you will. Whatever you make a MUST will happen. Say it out loud and write it down. *"I MUST change my life."*

"I MUST save my marriage."

"I MUST reach my kids."

"I MUST get a better job."

"I MUST start a business."

"I MUST lose weight."

When you MUST it, you'll make it happen.

This may be a totally new approach for you. It may feel uncomfortable and even awkward. Try it anyway. Do something different, anything different. The status quo is fatal. If you keep doing the same thing over and over, you'll get the same result over and over. Seize the day and possess the power of NOW.

People who keep getting what they want create an action plan. They know how to concisely and precisely state the goal they want. They are able to develop realistic steps to achieve the goal. Successful people reach outside of themselves and foster relationships with people who have the resources needed to achieve each step. Successful people can take and share responsibility for the steps toward a goal. They also know where (and when) the finish line is by setting due dates for achieving their goals.

My mother used to tell me actions speak louder than words. She was right. You can talk all day about what you want to do, what you are going to do, what you wish you could do, but it's all hot air and wasted time until you act on it. Gandhi said the future depends on what you do today. What will your future look like? What are you doing today to shape your future? Perhaps Carl Jung said it best when he said you are what you do, not what you say you will do. Successful people are doers. The Apostle James understood this principle and tried to motivate the early Church when he said, "But be doers of the word, and not hearers only, deceiving yourselves" (James 1:22). Successful people don't just listen to sermons, read books and watch motivational videos; they implement the skills, techniques and principles learned from those resources. What are you listening to? What are you doing to shape and define your future?

Successful people maintain a persistent mindset. Mindset is everything in success. Your mindset includes your attitude, convictions, and core beliefs.

57

These are what you are, deep inside. Your core beliefs are your true identity, your true north, the real you. Never betray them. Successful people live by their core. Gut-honest convictions guide their daily choices.

Yet even really successful people become weary with the grit and grime of the daily grind. The difference between the great achiever and the under-achiever is their daily routine. Go-getters know when to get away. They slow down and retreat for mental and physical rest. We all need to renew our belief system from time to time. You may be a naturally optimistic person and even a born encourager, but if you're around negative people all the time, you need to renew your belief system.

In his classic book, *The 7 Habits of Highly Effective People*, Steven Covey talks about sharpening the saw. This refers to taking the time to renew yourself in key areas, specifically spiritual renewal. High achievers take time to spend in nature enjoying God's creation. They slow down and meditate on their blessings. They focus on the positive aspects of life and seek balance and beauty in their lives. For this very reason, the Apostle Paul encouraged the early Church to "be renewed in the spirit of your mind" (Ephesians 4:23). The Old Testament prophet Isaiah told his people that "those who wait for the LORD will gain new strength; they will mount up with wings like eagles, they will run and not get tired, they will walk and not grow weary" (Isaiah 40:31). It's clear that successful people know how important it is to take time to renew their thinking.

When we do this, we transform our thinking from the tired, negative, and pessimistic outlook of the ordinary, to that of a great achiever–a doer! When the early Church faced tough times in ancient Rome, Paul stepped up with some encouraging words: "Do not conform to the pattern of this world, but be transformed by the renewing of your mind" (Romans 12:2). This is an interesting verse when seen through the original Greek language. The word *renewing* is translated from the original *anakaínōsis. Ana* means "up" and *kaínōsis* means "to make new and fresh." Successful people create time in their lives to make their thinking new and fresh each day, which gives them an upward momentum and direction.

You can't afford to disbelieve in yourself or the great achievements God has purposed you to accomplish. Great thinkers, great achievers, great men and women look up for their direction and find the spiritual *anakaínōsis* needed to succeed at higher and higher levels.

Action Steps

1. Where is your focus leading you?

2. Think back to your most recent success. What were you focusing on just before you achieved your goal?

3. What can you do *on purpose,* right *NOW* to make your goals a reality?

7: FOUR THINGS THAT LEAD TO SUCCESS

Success is nothing more than a few simple disciplines,
practiced every day.

-Jim Rohn

People who get what they want, when they want it follow a path to success. Along this path are milestones that mark the way toward their goals. These mile markers are critical to the successful journey of high achievers. The four mile markers are *disgust, desire, decision,* and *determination*.

Disgust

Satisfied people never change. Why should they--they're satisfied with their lifestyle, their

61

paycheck, their marriage, and the relationships they have with others. It is only when you become disgusted with your current condition that change occurs. Many are resistant to change because of anxiety and fear related to the unknown. However, when the fear of the unknown is eclipsed by the pain of the present, change happens.

What part of your life is disgusting to you? Is it your health? Is it your career? Is it the guy you're dating? Write it down and say it out loud. Let your ears hear it. What is in your life that is disgusting to you? When it makes you sick, you'll make it change.

Desire

Webster defines desire as something to long for, to hope for, to want or wish for. What do you desire more than anything? What is the ache in your heart? John Wesley traveled 250,000 miles on horseback, averaging twenty miles a day for forty years; preached 4,000 sermons; produced 400 books; knew ten languages. At eighty-three he was annoyed that he could not write more than fifteen hours a day without hurting his eyes, and at eighty-six he was ashamed he could not preach more than twice a day. Wesley had a deep desire to make a difference for God in this world, and he did.

Lou Nicholes, a missionary and author, tells a story about a young blind girl from France who was given a New Testament in raised letters. She was so excited and read it so much that the tips of her fingers became very calloused so that she could no longer feel the characters. She started crying because now she couldn't read the Bible at all. As she wept, she pressed the Scripture to her lips and was surprised that her lips were more sensitive than her fingers and she could actually read with her lips. She spent the night moving her lips along the raised letters of her Bible. How much do you desire the thing you long for?

During World War II, local inhabitants were used to build certain projects in Panama. This worked well for the military and the locals for a while, but the military began to recognize that the Panamanians would only work two or three days a week and then return home. They had made enough to meet their needs, so why should they work anymore? Arguments and negotiations were futile, and progress was reduced to almost nothing. After some thinking, an American officer decided to change tactics. He promptly ordered enough Sears and Roebuck catalogues for every family in the nearby community and had them delivered door to door. Suddenly, workers started showing up to the jobsite ready to work. The locals had acquired desires they wanted and were willing to work to buy them. What do you want most in life? How hard are you willing to work for it?

Decision

Decision is the trigger that initiates the mechanism of change in your life. Nothing happens without first making a decision. Mike Myatt, a contributing columnist for *Forbes Magazine*, suggests five steps in making a good decision. Take a good look at your situation and determine what is motivating your decision. What happens if you don't decide to change? What happens if you decide to change? What is involved in the change process? How will your change impact those around you?

Conduct a cost/benefit analysis of your decision to determine the pros and cons of taking this step. What is the change going to cost you? How will making this change benefit you, your family, and your mission in life?

Consider if this is the right change for your life right now. What is at the very core of this change? Are you changing for selfish reasons, or are you changing for the right reason? You can lose 30 pounds so the girl across the hall will notice you, but if you're married your change is selfish. Selfishness breeds controversy. Change is hard enough without fighting through controversy. However, you can lose the same 30 pounds to add 20 years to your marriage and be in the right. If you wonder if it's worth the fight, always choose right. Change made for the right reasons are lasting changes.

Publicize your decision to change. Tell the people you trust what your plans are and ask them to hold you accountable. You enlist the help of others by publically announcing your decision. People pay attention to your progress. Friends line up to support you. You effectively broaden you support base and increase your chances of success.

Make the decision. This is the most difficult part. Don't give in to analysis paralysis. Make the best decision you can, based on the information you have at the time. The best decision you can make is better than no decision at all. Many fear making the wrong decision and never experience meaningful purpose in their lives. I've learned over the years that change happens when the pain of the present exceeds the fear of the future. Don't let fear lead you by the nose. Ralph Waldo Emerson wrote, "Once you make a decision, the universe conspires to make it happen."

Determination

Webster defines determination as "a quality that makes you continue trying to do or achieve something that is difficult." I cannot express to you enough the power of determination. If decision is the trigger that initiates the mechanism of change, determination is the fuel that propels the machine forward. George Horace Lorimer said it best: "You've got to wake up every morning with determination if you're going to go to bed with satisfaction."

Kristi was a petite young woman with a passion for criminal justice. Although she was the only female in the class, she refused to be denied the chance to serve her community. She passed all her academics with flying colors, but the physical agility course was yet to come. She trained, ran, and worked out in the gym for weeks in preparation. The day finally came when all the cadets gathered to run the obstacle course, the final assessment of their readiness for police work.

The whistle blew and all the cadets burst into sprint, with Kristi leading the way. She paced each of her male classmates step for step. She successfully ran from station to station, completing the firearms portion. She ran the required distance in full sprint and under the required time. She dragged the 150 pound dummy the required distance just like the other cadets. Finally, after gaining the respect of her peers, she arrived at the 6-foot wall. It towered over her small 5-foot frame. She had come so far, too far to be stopped now. She jumped and reached, she clawed and scraped as the other cadets quickly climbed over the wall and left her on the other side.

The symbolism was too much for her as her throbbing heart filled with anger. She would not quit! She would not be held back! At last, she gained a small finger hold that gave her right foot a toe hold.

She strained to pull herself up to the top of the wall. At last she could see the other side to victory, but her strength was spent. Somehow, from somewhere, she lurched her left leg to the top and caught her heel on the edge. It was just enough to swing her tiny body over the top to success. On the other side, she could hear the cheers of her fellow cadets as she crossed the finish line. Her story reminds me of Winston Churchill's speech at Harrow School:

"Never give in. Never give in. Never, never, never, never—in nothing, great or small, large or petty—never give in, except to convictions of honor and good sense. Never yield to force. Never yield to the apparently overwhelming might of the enemy" (October 21, 1941).

It's not the strongest that wins, it's the one with the most determination. Never give up.

"I will" power. Results of the *American Psychological Association's annual Stress in America Survey* revealed that participants regularly cite lack of willpower as the No. 1 reason for not following through with such changes. Will Power is the ability to delay immediate gratification for delayed satisfaction. Kelly McGonical, Stanford University professor and author of *Maximum Willpower*, discusses three types of will power. "I won't" power-- the ability to resist temptation; "I will" power--the ability to do what needs to be done; and "I want" power--the awareness of your long-term wants and goals.

What in your life needs to be done? Name it, say it out loud. Let yourself hear it, and let others hear it, too. "I will" are two very powerful words. Just ask American paratrooper Arthur Boorman, who returned home from the Gulf War injured and suffering from chronic back and knee pain. He kept telling himself, despite medical records to the contrary, "I will walk again." His "I will" power resulted in the loss of 147 pounds in 10 months, and now he walks without crutches. Determination propels you forward to your highest levels of success.

Action Steps

1. What part of your life is disgusting to you?

2. What do you desire more than anything else?

3. What is motivating your decisions?

4. Follow Mike Myatt's five steps in making a good decision this week and see what happens.

8: THE EVIDENCE OF LIFE CHANGE SUCCESS

Success is not the key to happiness. Happiness is the key to success. If you love what you are doing, you will be successful.

-Albert Schweitzer

The evidence of true success is in your relationships. No one is an island unto themselves. You do not exist in your own world separate from others. Hindus believe that we are all connected to each other just under the surface. Like islands in the ocean, we look like we are disconnected and separate from each other, but in reality we are all connected by the ocean floor. John Donne, the great English poet of

70

some 400 years ago wrote,

> *No man is an island,*
> *Entire of itself,*
> *Every man is a piece of the continent,*
> *A part of the main.*

Like Donne's poem, your success or failure affects those around you. It is the modern narcissism of our culture that seduces us into believing we live unto ourselves alone. Success in your life is evidenced by the success you sow into others.

The evidence of true success is service to others. A recent study published in the *Journal of Career Assessment* found that people who are motivated to help others find greater satisfaction in their careers. Dr. Ryan Duffy, professor at the University of Florida, believes that individuals who use their careers to make a positive difference in the lives of others tend to meet their career goals. Successful people use their gifts, talents and success to serve and improve the lives of those around them. What pro-social components of your life can be used to make your home, job, or community a better place?

The evidence of true success is humility toward others. Truly successful people don't care who gets the credit for the positive change in their lives and the lives of those around them. If you want

71

to get what you want when you want, stop worrying about how your achievements can make you look good. If you look at the most successful people (Bell, Carnegie, Jobs, and Gates), they all wanted to make others' lives easier. They put others first. For example, consider the unconventional Golden Rule of Danny Meyer. His may not be a household name, but the CEO of Union Square Hospitality Group and owner of Gramercy Tavern, Union Square café, and Shake Shack has certainly fed many a family. His philosophy can be summed up in three statements:

If you don't take care of your employees, your service to customers doesn't matter much. Think about that for a minute. Your first line of advertising is your employee. Keep them happy and the customer service will naturally flow out from their job satisfaction. It's a simple equation. Whatever you think about, you begin to feel; whatever you feel, you do. If your employees are thinking, "Wow. My boss really cares about me. They stopped by my office to ask about my kid's ballgame"--that employee will begin to feel like they are important, needed and affirmed. The natural result is a healthy, confident, and happy employee interacting with potential customers in the community. Happiness is contagious! The customer begins to associate the positive emotion they contracted from your employee and apply that positive mood directly to your product. Presto! Your products make customers feel happy.

Prioritize who really matters. Meyer believes that every business has five stakeholders: customers, the community, employees, investors and suppliers. He prioritizes them in the following way: employees, customers, community, suppliers, and investors. Notice how he puts the employee first. They are his first line of marketing. Employees are going to talk about their job. Successful people understand this. By starting with humility toward others, the boss can impact what is being said about the company. People are either grateful or hateful. Employees can bash the company, or they can brag about the company. What marketing message do you want customers to hear? What reputation will your business have in the community? The ripple effect will eventually reach the investors, and you have the power to control what they hear.

How you impact others distinguishes your company. Meyer understands how quickly ideas can jump from his restaurant to a competitor's. Generating new ideas will always be a big part of business, but some of the best ideas are played out in the break room. What kind of impact are you having on your employees, staff, faculty, or family? How are you making a difference in the lives of those you work closest with? What have you done to market to your employees? What can you do stimulate the next great idea for your business? How can you encourage the creativity of your employees? Don't hog the spotlight. Let others shine and get some of the credit.

Life Change Success happens in the mind; evidence happens in the market place. When you begin to change the way you approach success, those around you are positively influenced toward success. When parents unify their hearts and minds, children behave differently. When bosses put the mental, physical and emotional health of their staff before the bottom line, customer service soars to new heights and the whole marketplace enjoys the benefits of your success.

The evidence of true success is in your circumstances. Life happens to all of us. Sometimes it's easy to look up at those who are "wealthy and successful" and be blinded to the pain they are experiencing. I remember hearing a man complain about how easy other people have it and how much they complain about life. He said, "I wish I was so wealthy I could be as miserable as they are." His statement failed to perceive the depth of their pain.

It rains on everyone. Perhaps you've heard that before. I think everything we need to know to succeed, we've heard before in Sunday School. I remember a story about the Apostle Paul's experience with persecution during the early days of the Christian Church. The background is found in 2 Corinthians 4: 8-9. Paul talks about four struggles he faced and survived.

Paul tells the Corinthian church how he was *pressed but not crushed*. In the original writing of this letter, Paul creates a word picture contemporary within the culture in which he is living. In the Roman era, prisoners would be laid flat on their back, and soldiers would place heavy, flat rocks upon the prisoner's chest. This was a slow and agonizing death that resulted in the eventual suffocation and crushing of the prisoner's ribcage and lungs. In the pursuit of your goals, you will feel pressed on all sides. Paul tapped into his faith to prevent being crushed by the naysayers and haters. What do you tap into when you feel the pressure? Is it powerful enough to help you push back and still have room to breathe?

Again, Paul writes to the church how he was often *perplexed but not in despair*. In your quest for success you will find yourself feeling perplexed, confused, bewildered and befuddled, but you don't have to become depressed or in despair. What you think about the longest becomes the strongest. Paul had a history with the God of his faith. This passage of scripture was not the beginning of his story, nor the ending. In those perplexing moments, Paul fixed his eyes on the prize! Successful people get what they want, when they want it, by rising above the temporary confusion and finding a way to reach the prize. Can you see your prize from where you are? Visualize it. See it in your hand. Ask God to help you reach it.

As we continue to explore Paul's quest for success, we find that he was *persecuted but not abandoned*. Success is born outside the box. History is full of people who were persecuted, laughed at and ridiculed because they had a new idea. Columbus' own crew wanted to kill him before they found the New World. J. K. Rowling, author of the *Harry Potter* series, was rejected by 12 publishers before Barry Cunningham from Bloomsbury agreed to give her a chance. Walt Disney's first animation company went bankrupt, and investors turned him down 302 times before he got the financial backing for Disneyland. John Grisham was rejected by 28 publishers before *A Time to Kill* was accepted. Stephanie Myers' *Twilight* was rejected 14 times before she finally found a publisher and $40 million.

Paul is careful to remind us that he was persecuted but never abandoned. He always had his friends, his faith, and his God. It's very important that you surround yourself with these three. When the world laughs at you and says, "It can't be done," turn to your friends, your faith, and God. You'll never be abandoned, and you'll always get what you want in that moment.

Paul may be an extreme example of epic success, especially, when he tells his readers about how he has been *struck down but not destroyed*. Most of us will not have to endure the overwhelming odds that Paul did. The government hated him, the church

76

hated him, and even the crowds hated him at times. Yet I still believe the principle is true. How many times have you been verbally struck down? Perhaps you're in a physically abusive relationship. You may be a victim of bullying and teasing at school. How many times have you been struck down? Count them. Say it out loud…. Now, how many times have you gotten back up again? How many times have you found within yourself the rebellious and defiant strength to get up one more time and reach for the prize? Count them. Say it out loud! *YOU ARE NOT DESTROYED.*

Later, in 2 Corinthian 4: 16-17, Paul talks about the reality of struggling for success in this life. He admits that outwardly he is wasting away. Success is not easy. It's hard to succeed. If it was easy, everyone would be a success. Yet even as he struggles against the obstacles, he feels renewed inwardly each day. How does he do this? Faith. Paul understood the magnitude of the great achievement he struggled toward, and he was very aware of his own limitations. He needed to cling to something bigger than himself. For Paul, that "greater power" was God. In my own struggle for success, God has proven to be a source of strength, comfort and courage in very difficult times. What is your "higher power?" Have you tried faith? Have you tried God?

Action Steps

1. How will you serve others today?

2. Who can you shine the spotlight of success on this week?

3. Happiness is contagious. How will you spread it?

9: THE ONLY THING THAT CAN STOP YOU: FEAR & DOUBT

The only thing we have to fear is fear itself.

-Franklin D. Roosevelt

A hero is someone who, in spite of weakness, doubt or not always knowing the answers, goes ahead and overcomes anyway.

-Christopher Reeve

It has been said that fear and doubt have sabotaged more dreams than failure ever could. These two partners in crime often work hand in hand to effectively short circuit millions of hopes and dreams. Successful people are not untouched by these two; instead, they have an intimate understanding of their

79

familiar tactics. If you hope to succeed, stop avoiding fear and doubt. Get to know them. Sun Tzu, the Chinese military general, strategist, philosopher and author of *The Art of War* once wrote,

> "If you know the enemy and know yourself, you need not fear the result of a hundred battles. If you know yourself but not the enemy, for every victory gained you will also suffer a defeat. If you know neither the enemy nor yourself, you will succumb in every battle."

In this chapter we look closely at the enemies of success: *Fear and Doubt.*

When you hesitate and question yourself, you give power to your doubt. I want you to take that power back. Let's start the process by defining the problem. Self-doubt focuses on your own competence until you begin to hesitate or feel uncertainty about fully engaging in life. It's like a bridle on a horse that reins back your success and pulls to the left or right of your dreams. When you let doubt control your life, eventually, you lose control of everything. I've seen powerful stallions that are under the total control of a rider simply because the horse has yielded to the reins. How does this happen?

When we focus on our perceived competence or lack of it, anxiety emerges. Like other negative mood states (depression, boredom, anger, fear, etc.) we begin to look for coping mechanisms for those negative feelings. When it comes to self-doubt, researchers at Ohio State University and Reed College have discovered five ways people cope with self-doubt. Braslow, Guirrettaz, Arkin, and Oleson (2012) found that people engage in either self-handicapping, overachievement, the imposter phenomenon, other enhancement or the stereotype threat.

Let's take a look at the first one, *self-handicapping*. When people believe that they will fail, they often engage in activities that actually ensure their failure. They do this so they have an excuse other than their lack of ability. Some people will "shoot themselves in the foot" to cover up their own perceived inability. It is often easier to blame the handicap than take responsibility for failure. In the end, the person never knows if they could have succeeded.

Overachievement is another way to self-sabotage. This coping skill seeks to exert overwhelming efforts to avoid failing. The overachiever attempts to plan, focus, create and answer every possible question from every imaginable angle. In doing so, they make the mundane and simple so multifaceted and complex it ensures failure. Their own self-doubt will turn any mole hill into Mount Everest.

The Imposter Phenomenon. This syndrome is indicative of those who believe their successes are not an accurate reflection of their abilities. When asked about their successes, they tend to downplay their skills and attribute events to "good luck" or "accident." Cognitive Therapists call this "discounting the positive." Even when they have hard evidence of their success, they minimize it and continue to suffer with self-doubt. In their own mind, success is unwarranted, and they don't deserve what they have achieved.

Other Enhancement. This approach allows the person to blame their failures on someone else. When someone misses their goal or outright fails, they can always blame the opponent or colleague for getting a head start, or the system for being rigged. This prevents an individual from totally sabotaging their own efforts by simply drawing attention to the unfair advantage of others. This insures that self-doubts will come true and responsibility for success can be avoided.

The Stereotype Threat is unique in that it taps into fears associated with core issues of identity, and identity with one's gender or ethnicity. For example, a woman faced with a repeated stereotype threat may give up hope of being good in math or science. Stereotypically, women are not perceived as being part of the sciences, and this bias can become deeply embedded in a woman's mind, leading to profound self-doubt. Likewise, some ethnic groups are perceived as academically deficient. People in those groups may face a stereotype threat and sabotage their academic success to avoid being racially inauthentic in the eyes of their peers.

These coping mechanisms are all driven by the need to measure up. We compare ourselves with others. We pull up at a stop light and compare vehicles. We move into a neighborhood and compare houses, landscaping, fences, pets and even our children. We are constantly trying to measure up to the next person. We all do it. Young, old, big, little, politicians, celebrities, and the poor all try to measure up to someone else. In his book, *Never Goin' Back*, Al Roker said even though he had a beautiful wife, three great children and a high power career, he still felt that he wasn't good enough.

What motivates this need to measure up? More often than not, it's the inner critic in each of us. It's the critical voice from the past that haunts the shadows of our minds and sabotages our success so often. Remember Sun Tzu the Chinese warrior philosopher? He would tell us to know our enemy, so let's take a closer look at this inner critic.

The Inner Critic capitalizes on the Thinking-Doing-Feeling formula. Since the Inner Critic is in your head already, he can really mess with your thinking. A few things you must remember about the Inner Critic:

He is automatic and subtle. He's always there and moves around in the shadows without being noticed. When something, anything, happens we react to the event based upon our thinking. The Inner Critic is always there to spin the event in a negative direction. He'll find a way to lure you into one of the five self-doubt coping mechanisms.

The Inner Critic has a "hair-trigger." Any little thing can set him off. It might be a brief memory, a familiar name, a smell, or even a single word, but that's all it takes for him to attack you with every self-doubt weapon at his disposal.

The Inner Critic is almost always irrational. One of his favorite tricks is what-if thinking. He lures you into trying to fill in the blanks, the what-ifs, and worry. Be careful. He's quick and these irrational thoughts and what-ifs may go unchallenged if you're not paying attention. If you're not paying attention and aware of what the Inner Critic is doing, you may totally accept these irrational beliefs as the truth.

The Inner Critic perpetuates avoidance. The longer you listen to the unchallenged irrational thoughts, the deeper you plunge into self-doubt and failure. You will literally create ways to avoid successful situations. This Inner Critic creates a self-fulfilling prophecy in your mind. You don't think you can succeed, therefore you don't feel successful, and then you begin acting (doing) like a failure.

The Inner Critic is persistent and if left unchallenged will breed minions to do his dirty work in your mind. These minions come in various shapes and sizes, but usually take four basic forms. Dr. Edmund J. Bourne, author of numerous publications on the topic of stress and anxiety, defines these minions as The Worrier, The Critic, The Victim and The Perfectionist.

The Worrier, according to Bourne, is the strongest of these minions. He promotes all kinds of anxiety and worry. *Worrier* gets in your head and creates fantasies of disaster and calamity. He capitalizes on the what-ifs that are already there and catastrophizes worst-case scenarios. *Worrier* keeps you up at night and distracts you from the present reality by dominating your thoughts with any sign of trouble.

The Critic promotes low self-esteem. He is always judging and evaluating your performance. He takes every opportunity to compare you to everyone else in the room. He will tell you that she is so much prettier that you or your coworker is much more successful than you are, or their marriage is perfect compared to yours. *The Critic* reminds you of all your past failures and keeps those failures in the forefront of your mind. He says to you, "You're so stupid. You can't do anything right." He may tell you after a big presentation, "You looked so foolish up there. You sounded like an idiot!" If unchallenged, *the Critic*

85

can sabotage your success at anything.

The Victim promotes depression and helplessness. She tells you that progress is impossible and that there is nothing you can do to change your situation. She often convinces you to blame your parents or childhood for the problems and struggles you have today. *The Victim* often uses *Other Enhancements* to justify and rationalize depression and failure. She tells you, "It's not your fault; you were born that way." She may remind you of painful past experiences and say, "See, if your parents had not been so cruel and mean you would be successful now." When you believe *the Victim's* blame game, it leaves you feeling powerless to change your life or situation. After all, you're broken. You're flawed and there is nothing you can do to change this. It's genetic. This helplessness leads to hopelessness and depression. In the end, *Victim* convinces you with the mantra, "I can't...I can't...I can't...."

The Perfectionist promotes stress and burnout. He is never satisfied with your efforts. Like a cruel task master, he pushes you for more, goads you to do better, and forces his insatiable agenda on your life. Should and Must are his whip and chain. "You should be thinner," or "You must be stronger," or "You should be making more money," or "You must provide more for your family." *The Perfectionist* is the go-getter inside of

86

you that wants to be the best it can be. He exploits a healthy desire for personal growth and turns it into stress and burnout. No matter what you achieve or how hard you try, it's never enough to satisfy *The Perfectionist*. Eventually, you are duped into believing that you're just not good enough to succeed in life, and you quit dreaming about the future goals you once had.

Along with self-doubt, fear can have a paralyzing effect on your dreams. Fear is a primal emotion that is rooted in your physiological fight-or-flight response. When a person is afraid, there is an identifiable and external object to be feared. Whatever it is that you fear is usually possible, if not probable. For example, some people have a fear of snakes. At some point in their life they may have had some kind of negative experience with a snake. Perhaps they saw someone, or they themselves were bitten by a snake. Snakes are certainly tangible and external threats (at least some of them) and getting bitten by a snake may even be probable (especially if you handle them).

What does all this have to do with failure or success? Many people fear failing. Earlier we talked about how people go out of their way to avoid failure by engaging in self-handicapping, overachievement, the imposter phenomenon, other enhancement or the stereotype threat. Believe it or not, some people fear success too.

87

Success brings change and for some, change is scary. It's not unusual to avoid or even fear change. Yet change can be very exciting. You may change jobs and find a new career that is more challenging, provides a better paycheck, and puts you in the company of interesting and exciting people. On the other hand, that new job may pull you from your comfort zone, it might require you to learn new skills that are unfamiliar, and may even pull you away from friends and coworkers you've known for years. Success, and the change it brings, can be frightening.

Success also brings responsibility. Luke 12:48 reminds us that "to whom much is given, much is required." When we think of success, we usually think of the perks that go along with the achievement of goals, the respect we receive from others, and the six-figure paycheck. Yet the more we are given, the more we are responsible for. Success brings responsibility, but many are not ready for that responsibility. It takes a great deal of maturity to handle the kind of responsibility required by success. A mature person puts others first, is always honest, even with himself/herself, and is willing to sacrifice their wants and needs for the betterment of others. Success requires a great deal of sacrifice from us, and that can be frightening.

Success broadens your horizons. Climbing to the top gives you a whole new perspective. You see the world around you differently. You see the world inside of you differently. Some are afraid of what they may see in others and themselves from that height. Once you climb above the tree line of your distractions and excuses, the view is spectacular. You will see things from that vantage point that you were not able to see before. Startling and humbling vistas that challenge what you once believed about friends, family and even yourself will span as far as the eye can see. This summit can be a place of fear and dread or a perch for new horizons and soaring possibilities.

Success can also be very lonely. This may be another reason some fear success. Very few people really achieve *true* success in their lives. Those that do are among an elite few. The very rich find themselves on one side of a widening gap between them and the rest of their friends and family. The super intelligent are often very lonely and yearn for intellectual intimacy with others. The status quo is easy, and it's crowded in the streets of mediocrity, but few breathe deeply the fragrance of real success.

Now that you know more about fear and doubt, perhaps you may have an advantage over your enemies. As we learn more about how to get what you want when you want it, we'll explore ways to overcome fear and doubt and make your dreams a success.

Action Steps

1. How do you engage in self-doubt?

2. How do you compare yourself to others?

3. What do you fear most about success?

10: HOW TO OVERCOME FEAR & DOUBT

"If you know the enemy and know yourself

you need not fear the results of a hundred battles"

– Sun Tzu.

What is fear?

The dictionary defines fear as "a distressing emotion aroused by impending danger, evil, pain, etc., whether the threat is real or imagined." By definition it is only an emotion, a feeling, an intangible by-product of our perceptions. Albert Ellis describes it as a result of how we perceive an event. Some event happens and you think it means something (perception). You give the event a meaning. In other words you give power (fear) to the

92

event. Fear is something you create in your own head.

I recall a story about Louis Pasteur's irrational fear of dirt and infection. It was so bad he refused to shake hands. President Benjamin Harrison and his wife were so intimidated by the modern electricity installed in the White House they didn't dare touch the switches. If there were no servants around to turn off the lights when the Harrisons went to bed, they slept with them on. Sounds crazy doesn't it? Yet what fears are you holding onto? Years later, President Roosevelt encouraged a nation during the Great Depression by saying, "The only thing we have to fear is fear itself." Stop giving the things in your life power over your present and future goals.

How does fear hold us back?

There is a reason to stop letting fear run your life. Fear short-circuits your dreams and goals. Fear holds you back from achieving greatness. It stunts your ambitions. During World War II, a military governor met with General George Patton in Sicily. When he praised Patton highly for his courage and bravery, Patton replied, "Sir, I am not a brave man … The truth is, I am an utter craven coward. I have never been within the sound of gunshot or in sight of battle in my whole life that I wasn't so scared that I had sweat in the palms of my hands. I learned very early in my life never to take counsel of my fears." What if Patton had been held back by his fear? What if the soldiers on the beaches of Normandy had been held back by fear? Fear is real, but it's not the real threat. The real threat is a lack of ambition. Thank God for men and women of ambition.

Fear is a liar.

Remember, thinking affects your feelings (fear). When you see something or an event happens, you apply a belief to that event. The boss has just called you into his office, and you ask yourself, "What is this about? Why does he want to see me? They just fired Roger; I must be next. Oh no! I'm going to lose my job!" Panic (feeling) sets in and you become fearful based on your perception or belief about the event (the boss wants you in his office). Yet most of us never wait to get all the facts before we start to fear. Can you really trust your fear to be accurate? For all you know, the boss may be inviting you to take over all Roger's old accounts. This could be an amazing opportunity to really show the company what you're made of and finally get that big promotion you deserve.

The object you fear is rarely as powerful as you first believe it is. I'm reminded of a story I read years ago as a boy. Maria Leach tells a great story about *The Thing at the Foot of the Bed*. As the story goes, an old man lived in a large Victorian house, built many years ago, and swore he feared nothing. Late one evening, after crawling in bed, he heard a bump in the night.

He startled awake and peered down toward the foot of his bed. There, to his terror, he clearly saw two large eyes staring back at him! He gasped in fear, reached for his shotgun and blasted the monster with both barrels. In an instant he cried out in pain as he realized the thing at the foot of the bed was only is own two toenails shining in the moonlight. Don't let fear keep you from a good night's sleep or a job promotion or starting your own business, or finding the happiness you've been looking for.

How do we defeat fear?

Do you believe in your dreams and the goals you want to achieve? Deep in your core are you positive that you can reach them? If you are, then tell yourself. Say it out loud. Your heart needs the encouragement. Tell yourself you can do this. I know it sounds simple, but it really produces results. Cognitive Behavioral Therapy suggests that our thinking influences our feelings and our feelings influence our behavior. Positive thinking will naturally result in more positive feelings, adding fuel to more positive behaviors. Such thinking alone cannot change your life, but it will change your perspective of life and how you approach the circumstances you find yourself in. The Apostle Paul told the Philippian Church, "Finally, brothers and sisters, whatever is true, whatever is noble, whatever is right, whatever is pure, whatever is lovely, whatever is admirable--if anything is excellent or

95

praiseworthy--think about such things" (Philippians 4:8).

You may not be able to stop the waves from crashing against the beach, but you can find the energy to surf. Donald Trump says, "Get going. Move forward. Aim High. Plan a takeoff. Don't just sit on the runway and hope someone will come along and push the airplane. It simply won't happen. Change your attitude and gain some altitude. Believe me, you'll love it up here."

Believe in yourself.

The Donald understood the real meaning behind his statement. You can't count on anyone to lift you into the sky to soar. You have to believe in yourself. Stop relying on others to motivate you, pick you up, and light a fire under you. Believe in *you* and do great things.

If you lack faith in yourself, how can anyone else believe in you? The greatest power in the universe created you in His image. You are genetically designed to be creative and life producing. Your fundamental elements are engineered to create life. Ask God for a little help, and He will catapult you into greatness. Don't fear what awaits on the other side of human mediocrity. Grab hold of God's hand, and let Him fling you into significance.

Doing so means taking a risk. According to Webster, a risk is the possibility that something bad or unpleasant (such as an injury or a loss) will happen. Yet it may be just as likely not to happen. You may ask yourself, "What if I fail?" What if you don't? No risk, no gain. Are you really satisfied with a stagnant status quo life? I'm not and I bet you're not either. After all, you're still reading this book.

Consider Jack Dorsey's risk when he cofounded Twitter. During a *Business Insider* interview at *Time's 100 List* he told readers, "I don't know if there is something that's the riskiest ... I'm scared every day. It's a good thing. You want to take big risks." Sara Blakely, founder of *Spanx* made the same list in 2012 and said, "I took my savings from selling fax machines and I put it into the business. I also did the before and after shoots of my own rear-end. I put my butt on the line, and it's paid off. Women appreciated me just being honest and saying, 'Look at my butt. Here's what it does.'"

Life is full of risks. You take them every day. Each time you drive to work you risk being killed or injured in an accident. That's why you wear a seatbelt. Driving is dangerous. Each time you go out to dinner you risk your physical health by eating someone else's cooking. You have no idea what's going on back in the kitchen, yet you take the risk and even pay for your loved ones to join you in this dangerous behavior. Every time you walk down the

97

street you risk being hit by a car, mugged by a thug, harassed by a panhandler, converted by a cult leader or even struck by lightning. I hope by now you get my point. It's really not the risk that you're afraid of.

Margie Warrell, bestselling author and contributor to Forbes.com, concisely describes why we run from risk. Her first observation is that *we assume that something will go wrong.* It's much easier to imagine the terrible than the triumphant. So, we spend the majority of our time and mental energy imagining, visualizing and fantasizing about the worst-case scenario. We terrorize ourselves with imaginary catastrophes, and naturally we run away, instead of focusing on what you can gain or what could go right. Take control of your thinking and purposefully imagine what your success will look like. Actively visualize how you will spend your profits and how those profits will improve your current lifestyle. Close your eyes and imagine how you'll spend those profits, how much more time you'll have to spend with your spouse and family, or where you'll go on your next exotic vacation.

Warrell also notes that *we tend to exaggerate the consequences of potential failures.* We engage in the irrational belief called "catastrophizing." We expect disaster to strike, no matter what. We hear about a problem and use *what if* questions. "What if tragedy strikes?" "What if I fail and go bankrupt?" You can see how these types of questions can magnify the smallest of obstacles and turn them into fire-breathing dragons.

I've lived long enough to know that most of what I fear will never happen. One technique I use in counseling is to ask my clients the very questions they fear the most. "What if you fail?" "What if these imagined consequences occur?" "What then?" "What will you do to navigate through them?" By confronting yourself with these questions, you may be surprised at how resourceful, creative, and wise you really are at overcoming the consequences, in the unlikely event they happen. Keep James 1:5 in mind: "If any of you lacks wisdom, he should ask God, who gives generously to all without finding fault, and it will be given to him." Even if they do happen, keep in mind that failure is not an end it is simply an opportunity to begin again. It is not the opposite of success, it is part of success. Proverbs 24:16 says, "Though the righteous fall seven times, they rise again…" Stop catastrophizing potential failures and get what you want.

Use your support system

No man is an island; no man lives unto himself. Success in life does not happen to us in a vacuum. Mike Myatt, contributor to *Forbes.com*, says, "Behind every success are significant investments and contributions by some if not all of the following people: family, friends, associates, protagonists, antagonists, advisors, teachers, authors, mentors, coaches, and the list could go on." Those around us are also affected by our success and our failure. As a clinician, I've work with a number of individuals that struggle with drug and alcohol addiction. Even in the most basic of treatment models, you'll find that developing and maintaining a healthy support group is fundamental to successful treatment outcome. In other words, people cannot maintain sobriety without a support system. Alcoholics Anonymous (AA) is probably the most well-known of support groups, but there are many more: Narcotics Anonymous (NA), Alanon, Alateen, etc. The common denominator is the recovering addict has someone to lean on and learn from.

To be successful in life, marriage, career, and ministry, you've got to surround yourself with supportive people who believe in you. I've been lucky enough in life to have two such people in my life. My grandfather had his share of failures, but the powerful words of encouragement that he spoke into me have never been forgotten. As he tinkered with the Briggs & Stratton lawnmower engine, we chatted about little, meaningless things like the weather and current events. The smell of gasoline and WD-40 stung my nostrils as he wiped his hands with a filthy rag. Grandpa looked up at me, peering over his dirty glasses and asked, "Jeff, what do you want to do with your life?"

The question was so out of place that it took me by surprise. "I-I don't know yet. I've not thought about it much," I lied. The truth is I had been thinking about it, but wondered how a clumsy, mediocre student, who is bullied at school could ever become anything great.

Without missing a beat he blurted out, "You can do anything you want to do. You can be anything you put your mind to, son."

I was stunned. How could he make such an audacious statement and then ask for a flathead screwdriver? I noticed my hand shaking as I handed it to him. There was something in his confident belief that was passed on to me that cool autumn morning. A pride swelled up inside of me, and I walked away with my head held a little higher after that day. If Grandpa believes in me, maybe I can become something great. He died a few months later, but he planted a seed of hope in me that just needed to be watered. Years later I would meet another very important person who would water and nurture that seed.

It was a cool evening as we stood on the sidewalk outside the house. Tammy and I talked of growing up and the dreams we had about the future. We had only met a few weeks before. She had her wounds and I had mine. Bitter breakups make for deep conversations. Still awkward in our new relationship, I thought about holding her hand but wasn't sure yet about her feelings for me.

She kept asking me questions about my life and goals, and looking back now it seemed more like an interview than a conversation. No matter, I was thrilled she was even interested in me. Her long blond hair and big green eyes were more than enough to keep me answering her questions. We talked about my parents' ministry and how I one day wanted to be a national speaker or even an evangelist. I couldn't believe I had said it out loud! How did she pry that pipedream out of my heart? I suddenly felt exposed and jerked my head around to see if she was laughing.

"I believe in you, Jeff. I think you'll do great things in the world." Her green eyes flashed in the glow of the street lamp above. Blond curls danced about the edges of her face as the cool breeze whipped around us. I think I heard angels singing in the background. My heart leaped up into my throat, and tears stung my eyes. Those words split the night sky like a comet. She just stood there, smiling at me like she believed it. My life changed that evening, and I married her.

Who is in your support system? Do you have a grandfather or spouse that really believes in you? Do you have a group of friends that are there for you when you need them? Most people don't. In fact, most people settle for who is standing around them at the time. You deserve a good, healthy support system. Those don't come by accident; they're designed.

Take a moment to write down on a sheet of paper the five people you spend the most time with. Go ahead, I'll wait……..

Now, look over that list. Who do you see? What are those people like? How successful are they? You are the average of those five people. You'll never be any more successful than the most successful person on that list. Support systems don't happen by accident; they must be designed.

According to the University of Michigan Depression Center and the Department of Psychiatry, a support system in your life can be very beneficial. They suggest that a healthy support system leads to better *accountability*. Being accountable to another can increase your motivation to achieve your goals and dreams. Accountability partners, members of your support system, often provide encouragement when you become discouraged and lose your focus.

University researchers found that a support system contributes to *increased mental and physical health*. Support systems help protect against not only depression, but cardiovascular disease, stress and Alzheimer's disease. Creating a support system can lead to *better problem solving*. When you share your worries and stress with other supportive individuals, they can provide a broader spectrum of solutions. The larger your support system, the greater the likelihood that someone in your group has lived through what you're going through and can provide you with helpful strategies. If you're still not convinced, consider the benefits of enhanced brain fitness. You may not like the idea of a formal support group, but any social interaction will do--men's group, church family, eating in a public restaurant, or just hanging out with friends. Socialization and spending time with others in meaningful conversation keeps you mentally sharp.

What are you doing to construct your support system? Who are you interviewing? What kind of character qualities are you looking for in a person? Successful people design their life success. They look at their life purpose and mission and then surround themselves with people and resources that will help them accomplish the mission.

Jesus Christ had a mission to complete while on earth, and he clearly stated it in Luke 4:16-21. He designed His life activities and interactions with this mission in mind. He handpicked 12 people to help him accomplish the mission. He looked closely at the characteristics of each disciple and strategically assigned them to specific positions in His ministry.

Using Jesus as our model, how active are you in designing your support system? What is your purpose? Who are you joining with to accomplish the mission? Do they have the character traits that lead to success? Choose your friends wisely. They will lead you toward prosperity or poverty. Be deliberate in overcoming your fear.

Action Steps

1. How is fear holding you back from your success?

2. What are some of the lies fear has told you?

3. How will you defeat fear today?

ABOUT THE AUTHOR

Dr. Jeff Logue was born in Dallas, Texas, and lost both his parents in a car accident when he was only six years old. Despite that terrible loss, he was able to overcome the tragedy with the help of faith and family. Growing up in the shadow of trauma, Jeff clung to his faith, family and the unyielding determination to make a difference in the world. After years of sacrifice and perseverance, he earned a Ph.D. in Counselor Education and has dedicated his life to helping others find success in the midst of tragedy and defeat. Now Jeff and his amazing wife Tammy are embarking on their next adventure--raising teenagers.

Together, they desire to create a place that anyone can come to be inspired, challenged, encouraged and changed! This new place is called LifeNub. Come and discover a place where anyone can make a difference in their life and the lives of those around them. Come and see what's happening at www.lifenub.com.

Jeff Logue

References

Chapter 1:

Hewitt, P. L., Caelian, C., Flett, G. L., Collins, L., & Flynn, C. (2002). Perfectionism in Children and Adolescents: Associations with Depression, Anxiety, and Anger. *Personality and Individual Differences, 32*, 1049-1061.

Chapter 2:

Kross, E., Bruehlman-Senecal, E., Park, J, Burson, A., Dougherty, A., Shablack, H., Bremner, R., Moser, J., & Ayduk, O. (February 2014). *Journal of Personality and Social Psychology, 106*, 2, 304-324.

Chapter 3:

Hull, P. (2013, Jan). Answer 4 questions to the get a great mission statement. Retrieved from http://www.forbes.com/sites/patrickhull/2013/01/10/answer-4-questions-to-get-a-great-mission statement/#2715e4857a0b846d56135e1c

Sapadin, L. (2013). The Importance of Validation. *Psych Central*. Retrieved on January 20, 2016, from http://psychcentral.com/blog/archives/2013/09/21/the-importance-of-validation/

Chapter 4:

Leisch, B.W. & Finley, T. J. (1984). The biblical concept of creativity: Scope, definition, criteria. *The Journal of Psychology and Theology, 12*, 188-197.

Menendez, D. S. & Williams, P. (2015). *Becoming a professional life coach: Lessons from the institute of life coach training.* New York, NY: W. W. Norton & Company.

Chapter 5:

DesMarais, C. (2013). 5 Reasons to Stop Checking Facebook at Work. Retrieved from http://www.huffingtonpost.com/2013/02/19/5-reasons-to-stop-checking-facebook-at-work_n_2717437.html.

Hiscott, R. (2014). Why You Feel So Bad After Spending Too Much Time of Facebook. Retrieved from http://www.huffingtonpost.com/2014/07/17/facebook-study_n_5595890.html.

Khadder, T. (n.d.) *10 Worst Time Wasters at Work.* Retrieved from http://insidetech.monster.com/benefits/articles/5667-10-worst-time-wasters-at-work.

Chapter 6:

Canfield, J. (2008, June 5). Keep your eyes on the prize. *Success*. Retrieved from http://www.success.com/article/keep-your-eyes-on-the-prize.

Covey, S. R. (2013) *7 habits of highly successful people: Powerful lessons in personal change*. New York, NY: Simon & Schuster. http://www.touchthetop.com

Chapter 7:

Stress in America: Paying with Our Health, (February, 2014). The American Psychological Association. Retrieved from http://www.apa.org/news/press/releases/stress/

The Churchill Centre http://www.winstonchurchill.org/resources/speeches/234-1941-1945-war-leader/103-never-give-in

McGonigal, K. (2012). *Maximum willpower: How to master the new science of self-control* [Kindle Version]. Retrieved from Amazon.com

Chapter 8:

Dik, B.J. & Duffy, R. D. (April, 2009).Calling and vocation at work definitions and prospects for research and practice. *The Counseling Psychologist,3*, 37, 424-450

Chapter 9:

Bourne, E. J. (2005). *The anxiety and phobia workbook* (4th.ed.). Oakland, CA: New Harbinger.

Braslow, M. D., Guerrettaz, J., Arkin, R. M., & Oleson, K. C. (2012). Self-   doubt. *Social andPersonality Psychology Compass, 6*, 470– 482.

Roker, A. (2012). *Never goin' back: Winning the weight loss battle*. New York, NY: Penguin.

Chapter 10:

Leach, M. (1981). *The thing at the foot of the bed*. New York, NY: Dell Publishing

Myatt, M. (November, 2011). Self-Made Man: No Such Thing. *Forbes*. Retrieved from http://www.forbes.com/sites/mikemyatt/2011/11/15/self-made-man-no-such-thing/#51c63f9331fb

Jeff Logue